Saga

A Solo Female Wanderer Hiking Guide

Saga, A Solo Female Wanderer Hiking Guide. ISBN 978-1-961878-09-9 for paperback. Copyright 2024 by Sarah Rowe. For more information about this hiking guide and others, email hi@solofemalewanderer.com

A portion of the proceeds from the sale of this guide are donated to DNT to support their work maintaining the trail system and cabins.

Introduction

I wasn't initially planning to do Saga when I went to Norway in summer 2022. I had only learned that there were more SignaTUR tours than Massiv a couple months before I left, and I had been planning to do Massiv for several years.

But two days before I was supposed to leave, DNT posted that Massiv was impassable without snowshoes and skis because of the cold spring. I wasn't sufficiently badass for that. So when I arrived in Oslo, I went to the DNT store and asked what hike I should do instead. They recommended Saga – thirteen days from Lillehammer to Snøhetta in Dovrefjell National Park.

And I loved it.

This is a great journey if you want to go long without super technical terrain. You're going through some of the most spectacular national parks in Norway, and as you hike north, you see more and more mountains in front of you. You go from pastoral lands near Nordseter to the high mountains at Snøhetta. It's a mix of serviced and self-service cabins, so you can hike without worrying about carrying food and a tent.

As DNT says at the end of the hike description – are you ready to create your own Saga?

Table of Contents

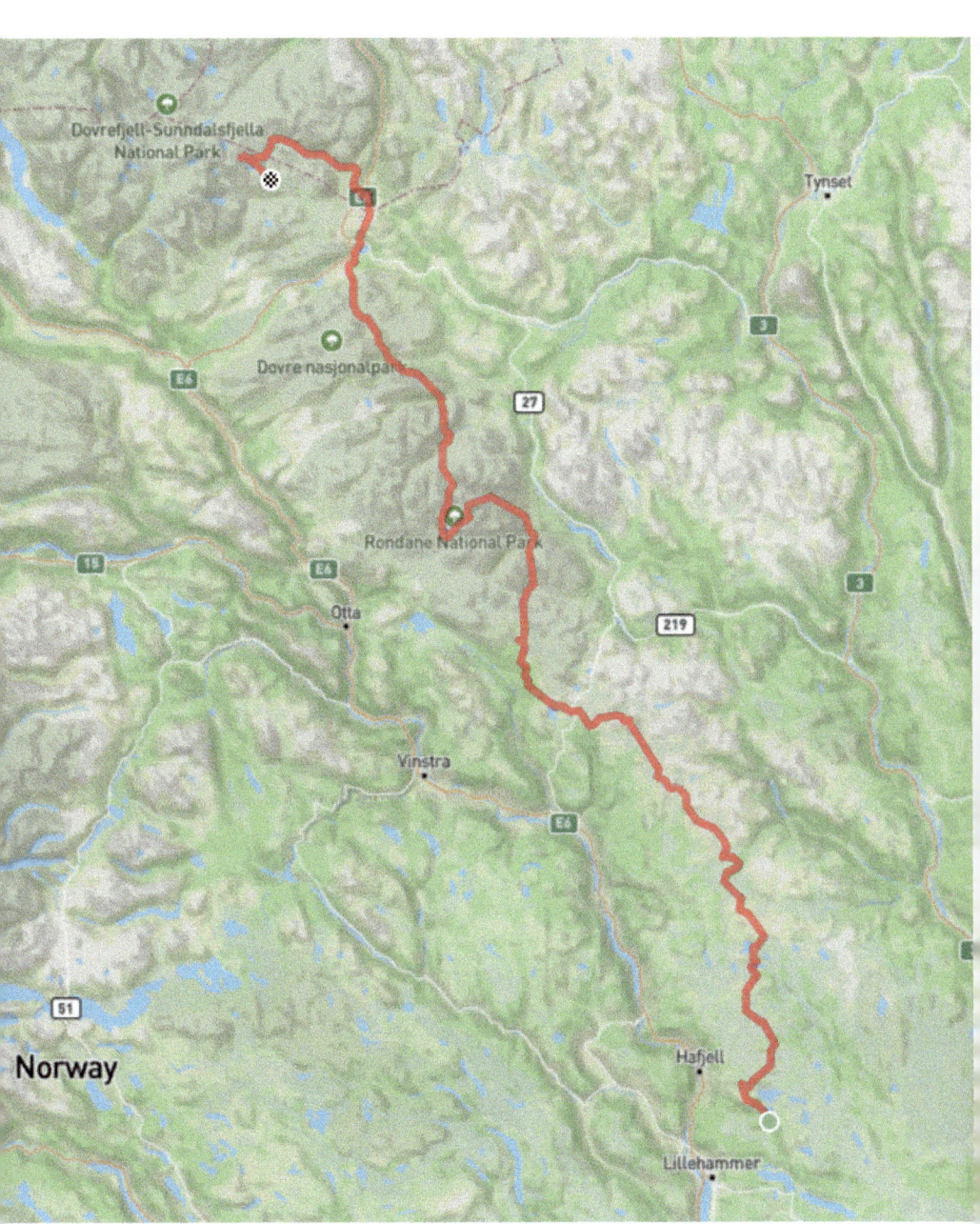

Norway

The Day by Day Plan

Hike day	Route	Cabin that evening	
0		Nordseter	
1	From Nordseter to Pellestova	Pellestova	
2	From Pellestova to Djupslia	Djupslia	
3	From Djupslia to Vetåbu	Vetåbu	
4	From Vetåbu to Jammerdalsbu	Jammerdalsbu	
5	From Jammerdalsbu to Veslefjellbua	Veslefjellbua	
6	From Veslefjellbua to Eldåbu	Eldåbu	
7	From Eldåbu to Bjørnhollia	Bjørnhollia	
8	From Bjørnhollia to Rondvassbu -- Option 1	Rondvassbu	
	From Bjørnhollia to Rondvassbu -- Option 2		
9	From Rondvassbu to Øvre Dørålseter	Øvre/Nedre Dørålseter	
10	From Øvre Dørålseter to Grimdalshytta	Grimdalshytta	
11	From Grimdalshytta to Hageseter	Hageseter	
12	From Hageseter to Reinheim	Reinheim	
13	From Reinheim to Snøheim over Snøhetta	Snøheim over Snøhetta	

Saga becomes steeper and more technically challenging in the later portion of the hike; the beginning has less challenging terrain, though long days

Length (km)	Elevation Gain (m)	Elevation Drop (m)	Time (ut.no)
-			
7.2	378	230	3.5
24.6	489	513	7
17.0	315	293	5.5
21.0	388	174	6.5
18.2	402	597	5.5
18.7	512	446	6.5
16.8	295	391	5.5
12.2	423	157	4
16.7	1,388	1,160	9
16.6	583	701	5.5
15.6	745	818	4.5
13.7	394	471	4
27.0	739	358	9
13.2	947	804	7

Nordseter – Pellestova

7.2 km
4.5 miles

378 meters
1,240 feet

230 meters
755 feet

3.5 hours
Moderate

The trip starts from Nordseter activity center, which is also the last bus stop on the bus to Nordseter from Lillehammer center. You start by following the road up to where the trail turns off, and then across planks over myr. (Myr translates directly as swamp, but it's a soft swamp - it's not a swamp like the Everglades, more like "watch where you're stepping" and lots of springy plants.) The trail is easy to follow, although there are some sections with rocks on the path. Eventually, you'll reach a clear plateau and then hit the top of Nevelfjellet - it's at 1,092 meters, and isn't a clear summit. From the top of Nevelfjellet, go northwest down towards Hundesetra, and then up the last hill to Pellestova.

My hiking notes

The hike today is really a warm up for the days to come. It's a flat and well-marked trail. There are a few sections with planks down over some swampier areas, but nothing technically challenging. Because of that, it's easy to do in the afternoon and spend the morning getting supplies from Lillehammer if you need to.

To be honest, I found this day a little boring in comparison to many of the days to come.

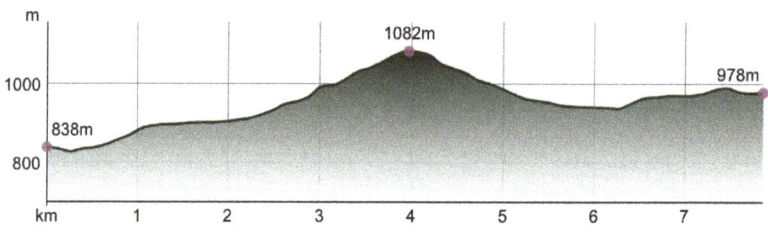

Pellestova is surrounded by agricultural lands, so you'll likely run into some sheep on the hike.

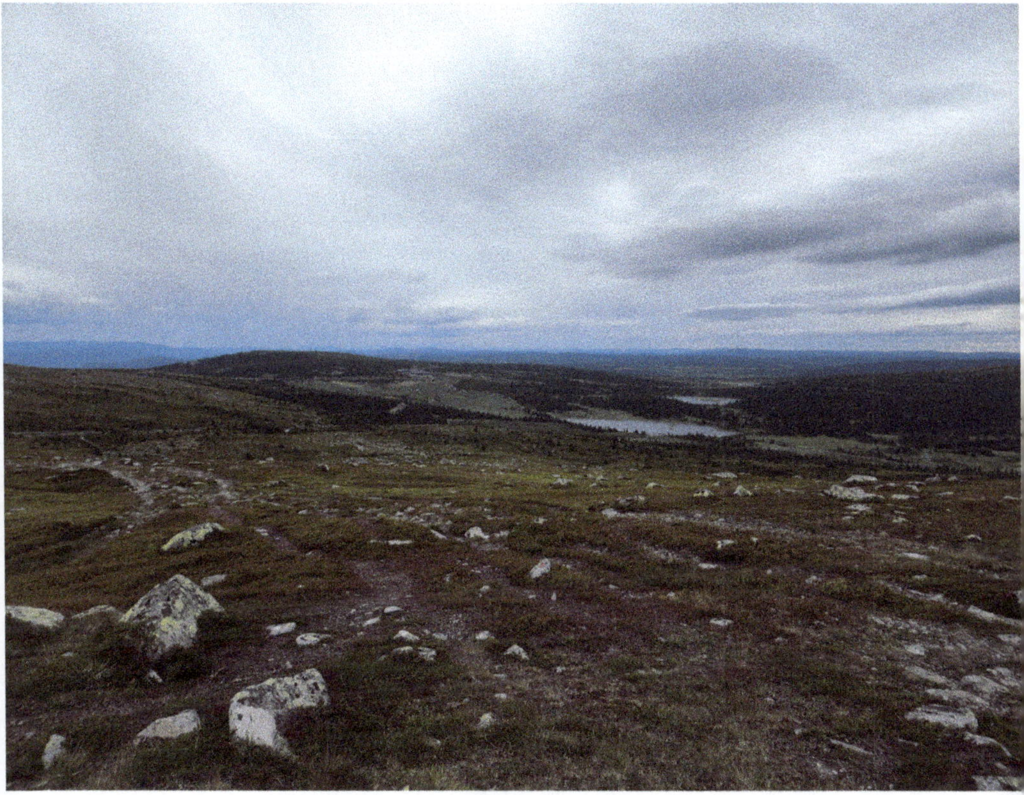

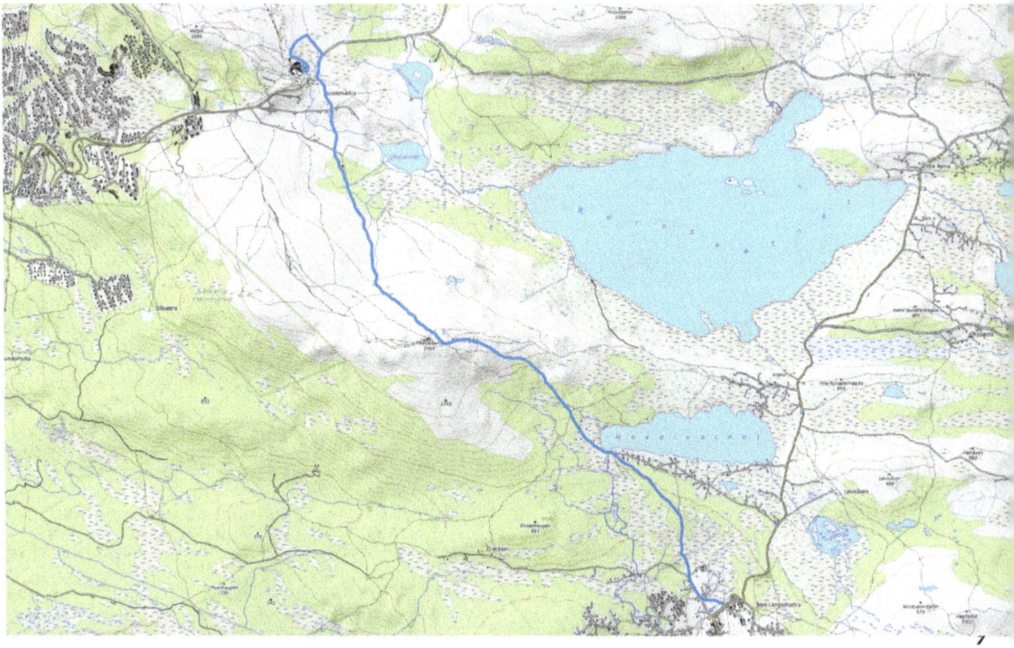

Pellestova - Djupslia

24.6 km
15.3 miles

489 meters
1,604 feet

513 meters
1,683 feet

7 hours
Challenging

The path starts below the hotel and then goes over construction and farming roads ("grusvei" in Norwegian) around Malmtjønnet. After there, there's a small climb up to Pellevegen, a road that you cross. There's a clear path through this area, and you'll follow it until you reach a bridge to go over Hitbekken. After that, it crosses Lie-Hornsjøvegen, another road, and then goes in between farms until you see a sign towards Djupslia. The path goes partially around a small lake to reach Djupslia at the end of the day.

My notes

There are several paths in the beginning of the day that look like they might be shortcuts on the UT app - they're not maintained, and I found trying to use them took much longer than sticking with the roads. The vegetation in the area grows really quickly, so trails easily become overgrown if they're not used.

This is another good day to get into the swing of hiking. I took it too fast because I was nervous about the weather, but it's technically easy and generally well-marked. The UT app was helpful for a couple of times where I wanted to double check that I'd found the trail after crossing a road, but there are generally T-marked stones on both sides of the road.

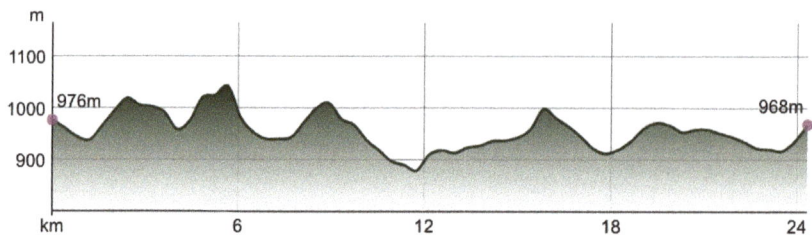

There are lots of sheep on the trail today, especially in the first half near the roads.

Djupslia – Vetåbua

17 km **10.6 miles**	**315 meters** **1,033 feet**	**293 meters** **961 feet**	**5.5 hours** **Challenging**

After leaving Djusplia, start by climbing up about 100 meters of elevation up to Åstkyrkja. After that, you'll start to go down through a forest, although there are some wet parts through here. After five kilometers, you'll arrive at Tauteren and start to have some gentle climb and bare rock again.

Keep going through here until you reach more myrlandskap (swamp landscape). Cross over the road and then follow the path through the wetlands to get to Vetåbua. This section can be a little confusing and is quite soggy, so make sure to follow the path markers and watch your step. Vetåbu is located slightly off the main road, and there's a small sign pointing towards it. UT is helpful if you miss the sign.

My hiking notes

The terrain is easy throughout this section. If it's rained recently, it can be soggy, and I found my poles helpful for poking the terrain to see if it was safe to step on.

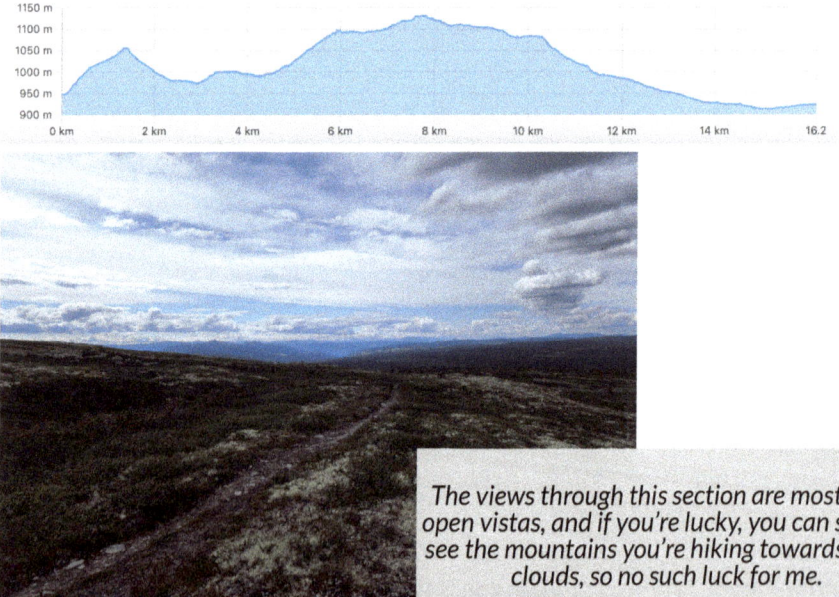

The views through this section are mostly big open vistas, and if you're lucky, you can start to see the mountains you're hiking towards. I had clouds, so no such luck for me.

First bridge of the hike!

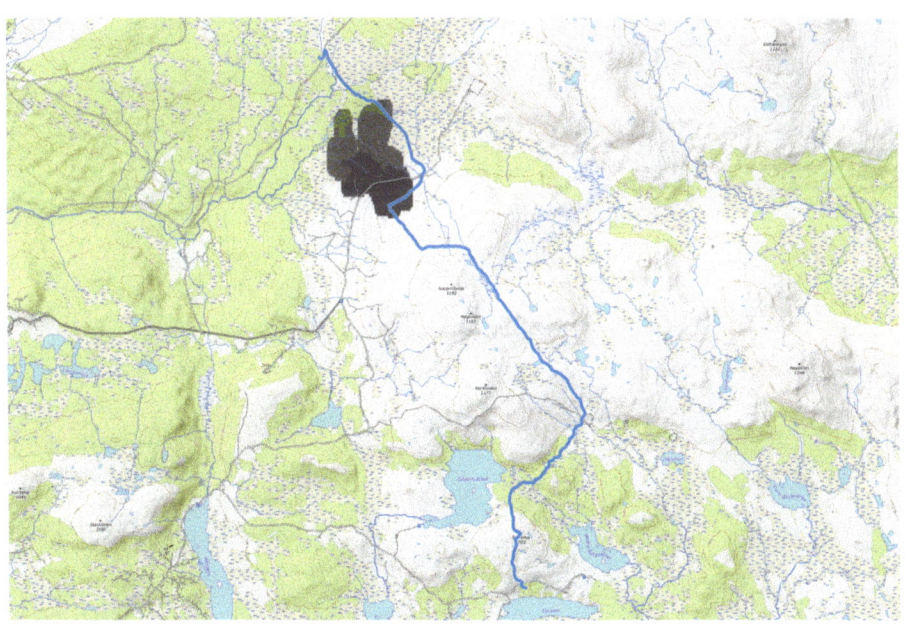

Vetåbua – Jammerdalsbu

21.0 km
13.0 miles

388 meters
1,273 feet

174 meters
571 feet

6.5 hours
Challenging

Today's first five kilometers go through a forest of Norwegian mountain birch, with some sections of myr again. (There is a lot of myr on the first half of Saga.) After this, the path starts to go up on bare rock to the highest point of the hike so far, Øverlihøgda at 1,170 meters above sea level. There's a drop down to Saubu and then a climb back up towards Jammerdalsbu, located at 1,130 meters. This section is exposed and can be windy - and make sure to take the time to avoid the wet parts of the trail.

My hiking notes

This was a tougher day for me because of the weather. There aren't a lot of trees to block the wind on this section, and I had a day with strong winds and rain. The rain also meant that the trail was soggy in parts, and my shoes got wet towards the beginning of the day.

If it's dry, it's doable in trail runners. If it's been raining, wear waterproof shoes and/or socks and rain pants.

Can you see any civilization here? Me neither.

Store Kvia
1350
Veslefjellet

m
1100
900
km
5
10
15
20
919m
1165m
1139m

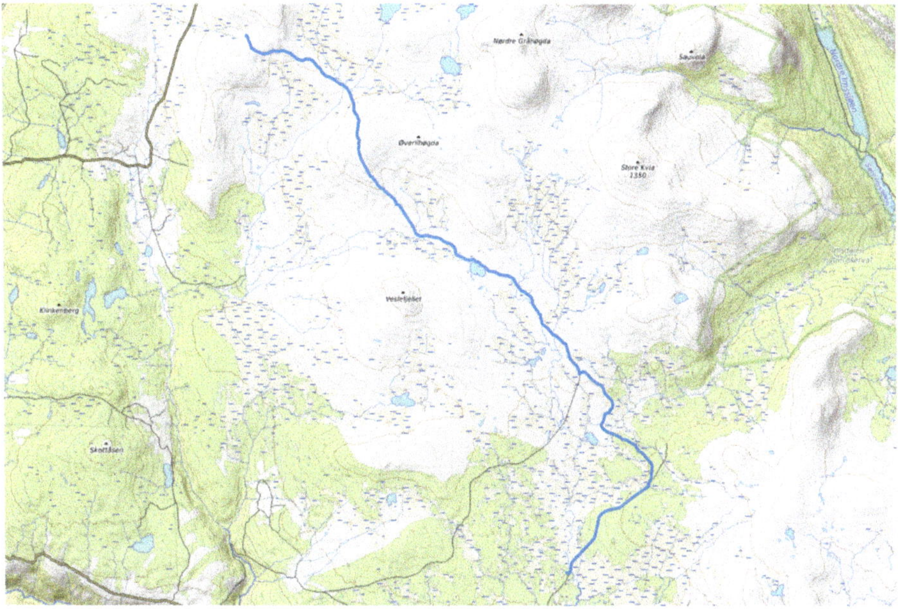

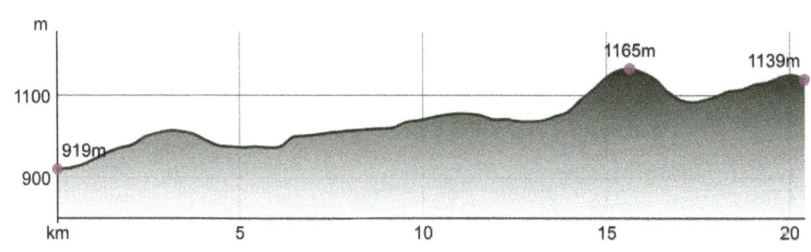

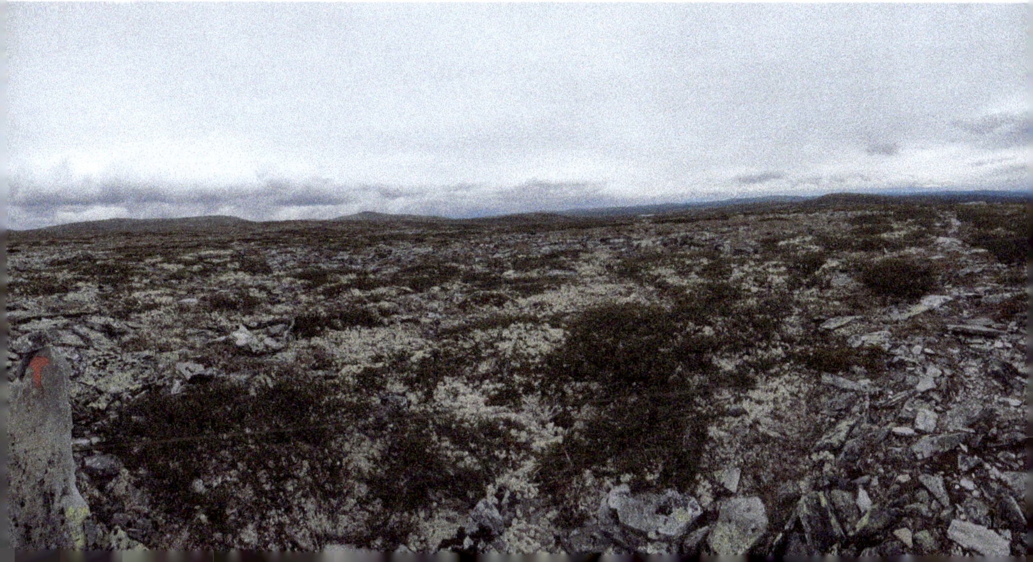

Jammerdalsbu – Veslefjellbua

18.2 km	402 meters	597 meters	6 hours
11.2 miles	1,319 feet	1,959 feet	Challenging

From behind the cabin, the trail starts with a short climb up and then gently down towards a road, the Friisvegen. Cross the road, and you'll continue to walk through myr. The terrain is relatively flat through this section, and if the weather cooperates, there are great views out towards Rondane.

Eventually, you'll reach a river that may need to be waded across depending on the amount of rain. After crossing that river, you'll spot a gorge on your left. After you pass the gorge, you'll turn up towards Veslefjellet, summit Veslefjellet, and then start the hike down on the north side. You'll reach the cabin shortly after the summit.

There is an old cabin called Gråhøgdbu in this area that is being taken down to restore wild reindeer habitat. Make sure to follow the signs to Veslefjellbua and not Gråhøgdbu.

My hiking notes

Today's path is part of the Rondanestien, which goes from Oslo to Rondane National Park. If you get nice weather, you should be able to see some good views of Rondane's high mountains in the distance. I didn't get nice weather, so that wasn't an option for me.

This was my first river crossing experience. The more experienced Norwegians around me took off their shoes, while I tried to hop across with my boots on. I was somewhat successful, but when I got to the cabin, the Norwegians were cooking dinner with dry feet.

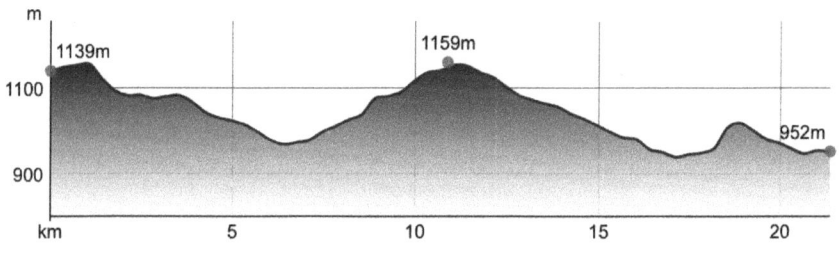

Starting to spot some mountains in the distance!

Veslefjellbua – Eldåbu

| 18.7 km | 512 meters | 446 meters | 6.5 hours |
| 11.6 miles | 1,680 feet | 1,463 feet | Challenging |

The path starts by going northwest from the cabin. The trail is easy to spot and to traverse, generally dirt without too many rocks. You'll also get a break from the myr from the past few days. After thirty minutes or so, you'll cross a road near a parking lot called Saltashaugen. You'll follow a road to Spidsbergseter, where you can stop at a cafe if you're craving warm food. When you reach the main hotel entrance in Spidsbergseter, turn to the right and follow the road towards the alpine ski area. You'll climb up a small ski mountain with great views around you, then start to slowly drop down to Storkvanndalen.

From here, the path goes up again, still with great views. You'll start walking into the forest and go past a number of small cabins. This is easy to traverse and a nice hike. You'll eventually cross a year round bridge that you climb up to slightly.

After this, you'll reach an area called Venåssætra. The path can be a little hard to find in this area, so make sure to check UT as you go. You have to follow the road until you pass the cabins, then turn off to the left onto the trail again. From here, it's about an hour left to Eldabu on easy trails.

Hiking notes

I finally got to see the mountains of Rondane today! I had cloudy and often rainy weather for the first few days, and I actually put sunscreen on. On the other hand, I wasn't able to find the promised bakery and cafe, so no fresh bread for me.

The most impressive part of this section for me was how alone I felt - there were large sections where I saw no other people and no signs of civilization. I saw a few cows and sheep, but that was about it.

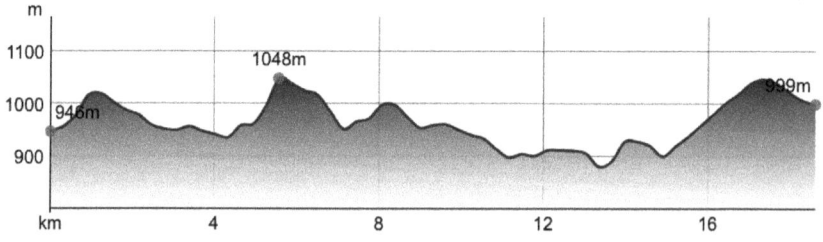

This is the last day with a lot of myr. Myr is a Norwegian bog found in the mountains, and it can be very soggy to hike through if it's rained recently.

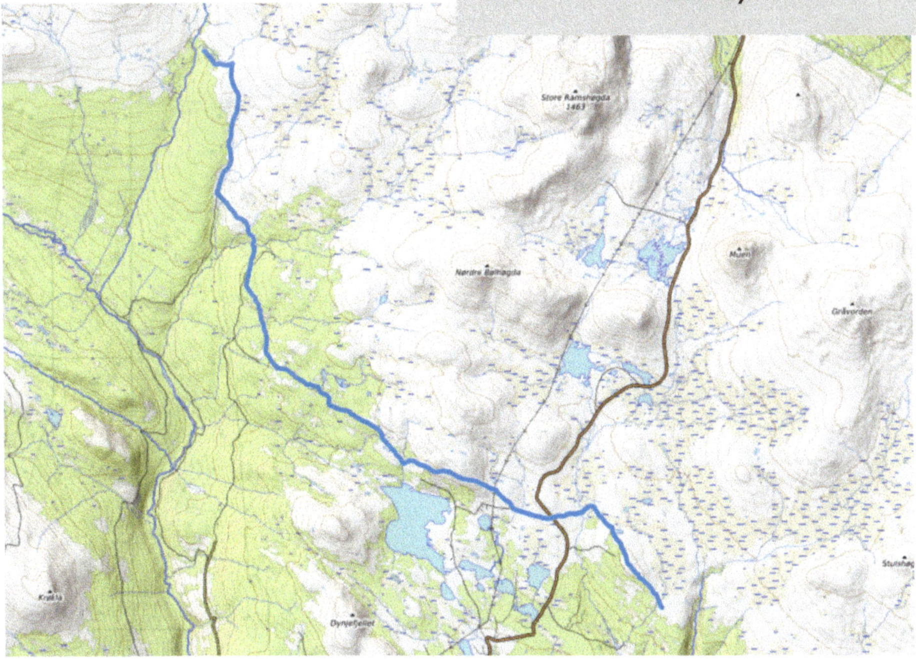

Eldåbu – Bjørnhollia

| 16.8 km | 295 meters | 391 meters | 5.5 hours |
| 10.4 miles | 968 feet | 1,283 feet | Challenging |

Today is two firsts: the first time that you'll be in a valley for a large part of the day, and the first time that you'll end the day at a serviced DNT cabin (yay, showers!). The path leaves Eldåbu and goes to the north. There are views of the mountains on both sides, and the path is mostly dirt, with a few rocks scattered in. After about two thirds of the hike, generally between ten to eleven kilometers hiked, you'll start to hike up the side of a mountain. After about a hundred meters of elevation again, the path starts to go down towards Bjørnhollia, then cross a river and go up slightly to reach the cabin.

My notes

This was an easy section, both technically and in terms of elevation. The trail climbed gently until the very end, with great views and not too many rocks on the trail. The challenge for me was underestimating the climb at the end. It felt much more steep and difficult than it actually was.

I was nervous about staying in the first serviced cabin of the trip, but it turned out to be fantastic. I'm torn whether the drying room for clothes or the fresh bread at breakfast was more exciting. Because there was assigned dinner seating, I skipped the awkward part of figuring out where to sit at dinner and got to meet people.

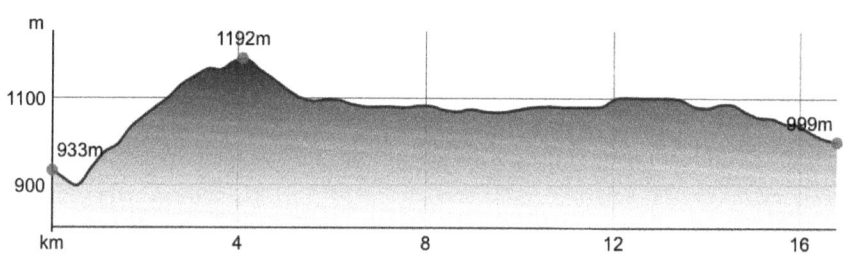

There's no phone service at Bjørnhollia itself, but there is phone service around it. I recommend stopping on the way in and checking the weather or answering any messages you need to.

Bjørnhollia – Rondvassbu

🥾	↗	↘	🕐
12.2 km 7.6 miles	423 meters 1,388 feet	157 meters 515 feet	4 hours Moderate
16.7 km 10.4 miles	1,388 meters 4,554 feet	1,160 meters 3,806 feet	9 hours Challenging

There are two options for today, depending on how many summits you want to conquer. If you want to go along the ridge line, you'll go up Langglupdalen, over Rondslottet (2,178 meters) and Vinjeronden (2,044 meters), before you start the drop down to Rondvassbu. This hike takes 8-10 hours.

If you're looking for an easier option, or for a rest day after already hiking for seven days, you can choose a path that goes through Illmanndalen. This is an easy to traverse path that goes along a lake before reaching Rondvassbu at 1,173 meters.

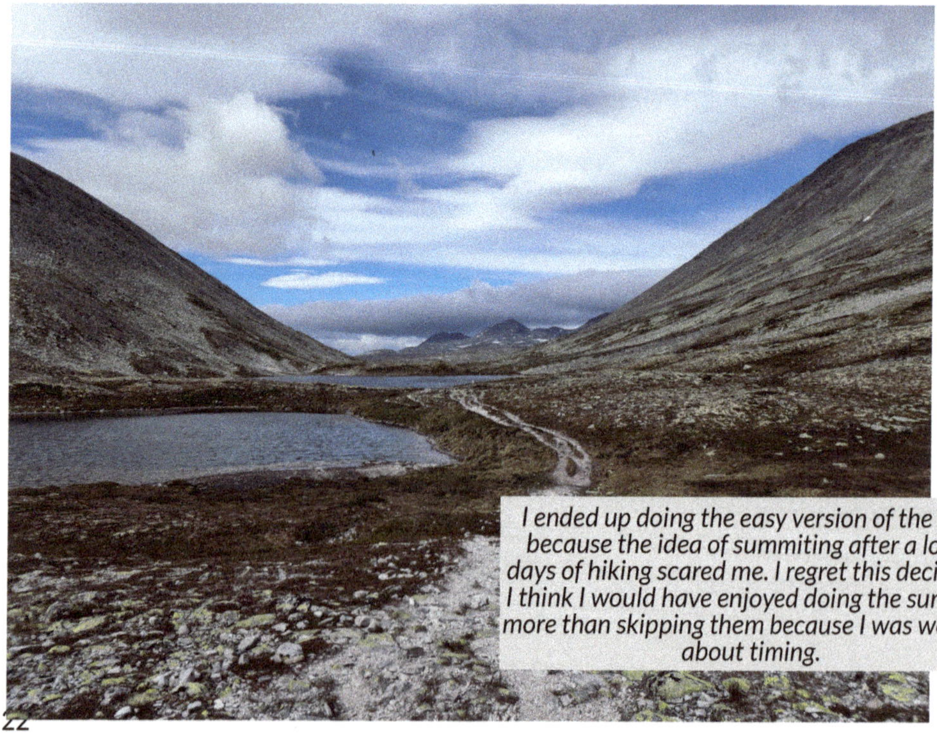

I ended up doing the easy version of the hike because the idea of summiting after a lot of days of hiking scared me. I regret this decision. I think I would have enjoyed doing the summit more than skipping them because I was worried about timing.

1300m
1100m
900m
1165m
1282m
932m
km
3
6
9
12

2100m
1700m
1300m
900m
2136m
939m
1164m
km
4
8
12
16

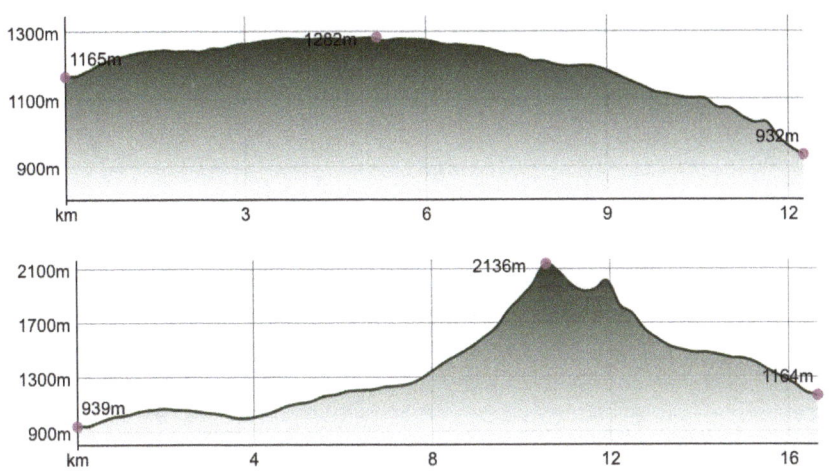

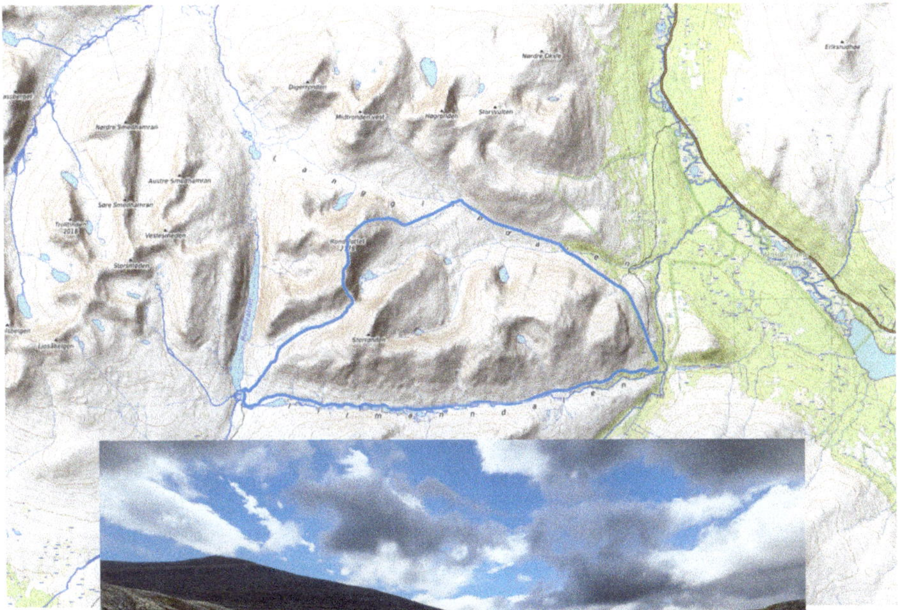

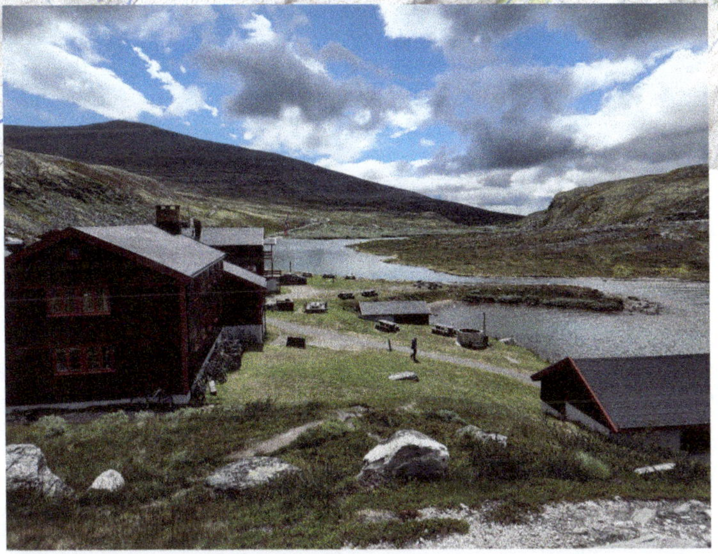

Rondvassbu – Øvre Dørålseter

16.6 km	583 meters	701 meters	5.5 hours
10.3 miles	1,913 feet	2,300 feet	Challenging

Welcome to the heart of Rondane National Park! As you look around on today's hike, you'll see high mountain tops and impressive valleys. Follow the path on the west side of the Rondvatnet (Rond lake), which starts to climb up towards a ridge. The path starts out dirt and changes into rock as you gain elevation. Once you reach the top of the ridge, it's mainly rock. You'll drop down the other side of the ridge, being careful to watch your footing on loose rock. (This section can be windy, so you may want to stop and put on a jacket while you're still on the flatter section). After this, the trail passes along a lake and then through a forested area with rivers until you reach Øvre Dørålseter at 1,070 meters.

Note: There's both Øvre Dørålseter and Nedre Dørålseter here, and you can spend the night at either. They are not DNT-run cabins but accept the DNT membership and follow the same price list.

My hiking notes

The map on UT shows a summer route that goes through the lake. Do not trust it. This is a boat route that you can catch from Rondvassbu, not a trail. It says something about how long I'd been hiking that this confused me. ("What, you mean I can't walk across the water?")

There's limited phone service at Øvre Dørålseter (I could only get it sitting outside under the flag pole), so send messages and check weather during the day. And check out the coffee taps in the wall of the dining room at breakfast - one of my favorite little things on the route.

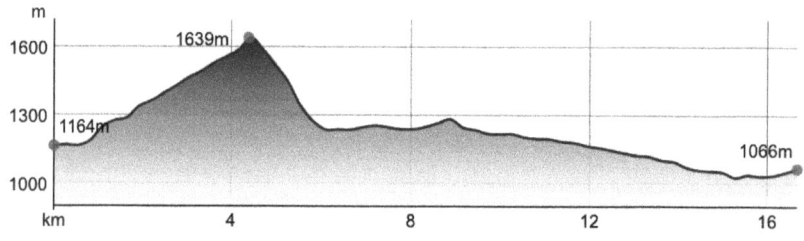

The hike has a huge variety of landscapes. The day starts with a climb over a rocky ridge, then by mountain lakes, then through forests into agricultural land.

Dørålseter – Grimsdalshytta

15.6 km
9.7 miles

745 meters
2,444 feet

818 meters
2,684 feet

4.5 hours
Challenging

Today's hike starts going up a bowl behind Øvre Dørålseter. The trail isn't too rocky, although there may be some rocky sections as you get close to the ridge. Once you reach the ridge, you'll start dropping down. If you've got clear weather here, you can actually see Snøhetta in the distance. After crossing a bridge, the path climbs slightly towards Grimsdalshytta. This part of the trail is mainly dirt and well-marked. There's a small final climb towards Grimsdalshytta, which sits at 1,000 meters above sea level with views across all of the Grimsdalen (Grims valley).

My notes

I started to notice the change in the terrain through this section - I was no longer at the beginning of the hike, going through myr and flat landscapes. This might have been my favorite day on Saga because of it.

Today also taught me the importance of slowing down and taking some cabin naps. Saga can be deceptive because there aren't ten or twelve hour days, and I hadn't realized how much I needed a day to relax. If I did it again, I'd factor in more rest time.

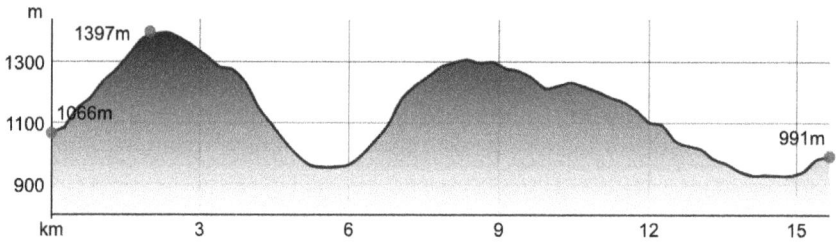

Grimsdalshytta – Hageseter

13.7 km
8.5 miles

394 meters
1,293 feet

471 meters
1,545 feet

4 hours
Challenging

Today's hike takes you out of Rondane and into the last section of the hike, Dovrefjell. The path starts at the back of the cabin, with a gentle climb on dirt paths. The path then starts a climb over a saddle, where there's some rock hopping as you reach the top.

After this, the path drops down to Hageseter. You can either pause here or continue on a dirt, relatively flat path towards Hjerkinn Fjellstue. The path to Hjerkinn Fjellstue can be tricky to find, since there are several options going through a series of farm fields.

You can also continue to Kongsvold and spend the night there if you want. I chose to do that in order to shorten the hike the next day. That extension goes over the king's way, and you'll retrace your steps slightly the next morning to continue up towards Reinheim. The path is dirt and easy to walk on, but longer than it looks on the map.

My notes

Navigation today can be a little tricky in parts - not because the trails aren't marked, but because there are several intersections where numerous trails come together, as well as sections through farms. I used UT a lot to make sure that I wasn't heading off in the right direction, which was very helpful.

If you want to pick up food or supplies, there are some small shops at Hageseter. Hjerkinn also has a couple of small shops with limited hours. If you want to add a rest day, you can take a musk ox safari from here.

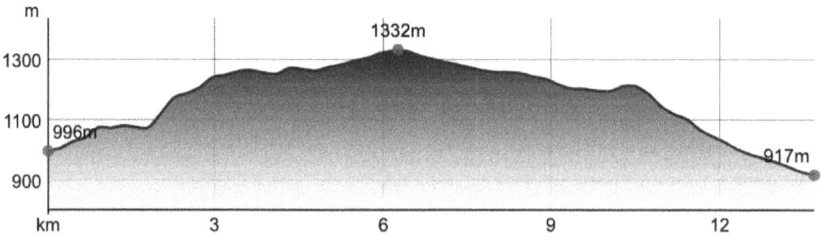

Avsjøen
Møhøe
Storhøe
Avsjøhøe
Pikhetta
Falketind
Gråhøe
1683
Fallfosshøe
Mesæterhøe
1425
Halvfarhøe
1687
Kattuglehøe

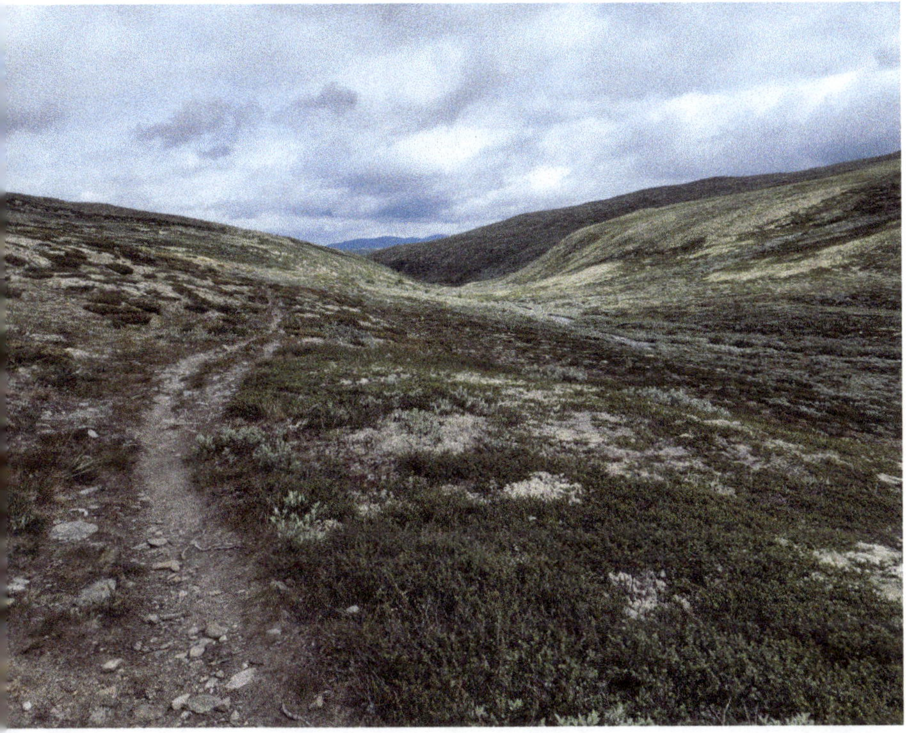

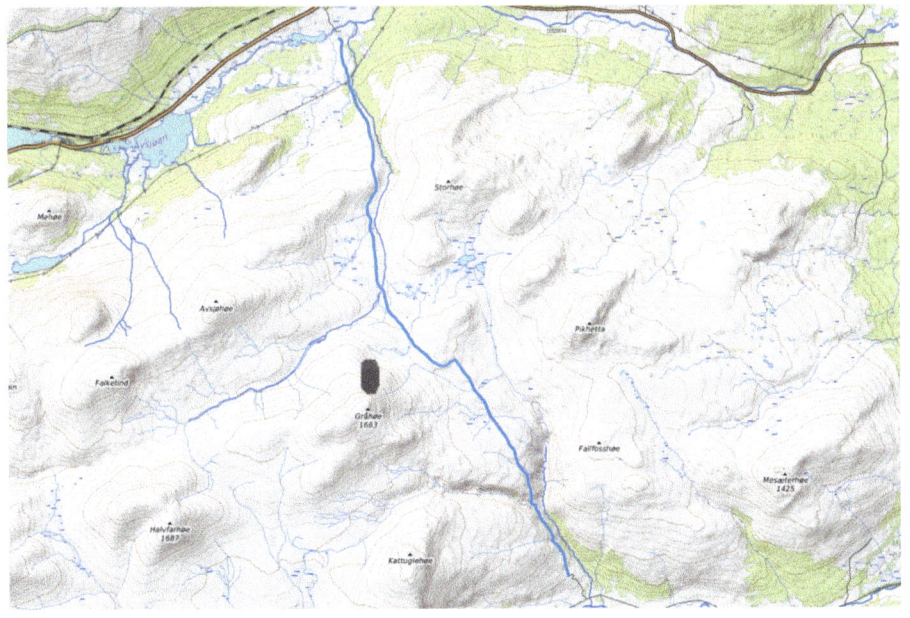

Hageseter or Hjerkinn Fjellstue – Reinheim

27.0 km
16.8 miles

739 meters
2,425 feet

358 meters
1,175 feet

9 hours
Challenging

Today's hike starts by going on the old king's path (kongvei) towards Grønbakken and Kongsvold. After several kilometers going on a dirt path towards Kongsvold, the path crosses the E6 highway and the train tracks, then goes over a bridge over the Kaldvella. (If you are starting the day from Kongsvold, you will turn to retrace your steps to reach the cross under the train tracks.)

About 2.5km after that, the trail meets up with the trail from Kongsvold and starts the climb up through the Stroplsjødalen. The trail goes along the north side of the Stropla river, but far enough from the river that the trail was dry when I did it. It's 17 kilometers of gentle climb up to Reinheim at 1,340 meters, mostly on dirt.

My notes

This section felt easier than I was expecting from the map. There's plenty of elevation gain, but it's slow enough that it never felt overly difficult. There are plenty of places to fill up a water bottle, so no need to carry a ton of water with you.

The views around me as I hiked up were fantastic - there were so many good spots to stop and have a coffee break that it was almost impossible to choose.

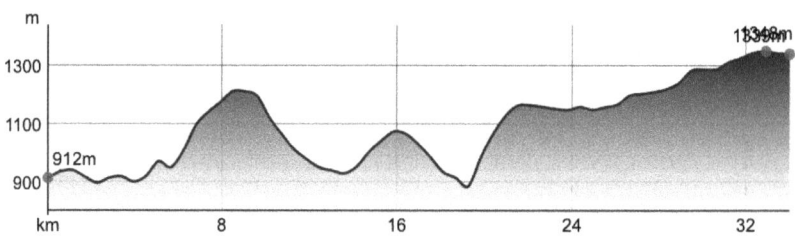

Note: the elevation profile goes from Hageseter; the hike is shorter if you leave from Hjerkinn or even Kongsvold.

There are essentially three variations of this hike, starting from Hageseter, Hjerkinn Fjellstue, or Kongsvold. The best way to think of is that the distance between day 11 and 12 is 40.7km, and you have different options on how to distribute that hiking.

Reinheim – Snøheim

13.2 km
8.2 miles

947 meters
3,107 feet

804 meters
2,638 feet

7 hours
Challenging

It's the last day of the hike! From Reinheim, follow the marked path up to Snøhetta at 2,286 meters. This is a very rocky section, and once you start the climb up to Snøhetta, you'll be scrambling over rocks. I had to put my poles away and use my hands. The trail is marked with sticks in sections, and it can be a little hard to follow - but there are usually enough people that you can follow the crowd.

Stop and enjoy the view from the top, then turn and head down towards Snøheim. As you start to go down, make sure to choose the path on the right, which leads towards Snøheim - otherwise, you'll end up back at Reinheim. It's rocky for the first two thirds, then dirt. Once you arrive at Snøheim, stop and enjoy the views over Dovrefjell!

My notes

How difficult today is really depends on how comfortable you are with rock scrambling. I think it's fun, so I was able to make great time. If you aren't great with balance, this will be a very tough day. You can always hike on the direct trail from Reinheim to Snøheim and then summit from Snøheim if you're worried about pacing.

This hike is really the perfect end to Saga, though. From Snøhetta, you can look back at all the places you've hiked to get there. I was so proud of myself standing at the top in the wind, looking around and realizing how far I'd come.

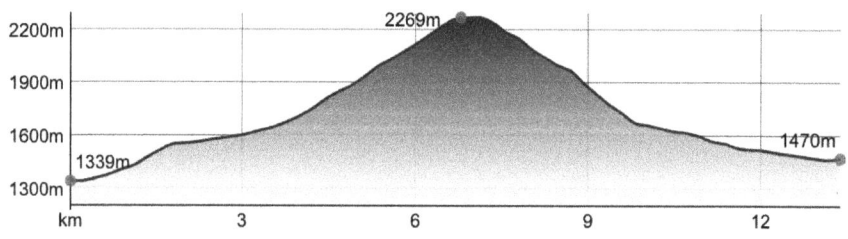

Route Extensions

Looking to add some more cabins to your trip, or want to conquer a few more peaks on the way? Saga doesn't have many additional cabin to cabin days that can be added to the hike - instead, the best way to add days is to spend longer in some of the cabins and do summit trips in the nearby area. Snøheim and Rondvassbu are the best for that and have numerous summits in the area.

These are a few potential extensions that you can add to the hike. It's worth asking around at the cabins as well to see what people have done and what's best with the weather conditions.

Route	Leaving From	Length (km)	Elevation Gain (m)	Elevation Drop (m)	Time (ut. no)
Åmotdalshytta	Reinheim or Snøheim	29.5	1,030	1,028	12
Summit trip to Storronden	Rondvassbu	8.5	959	959	4
Summit trip to Veslesmeden	Rondvassbu	11.8	838	838	4
Summit trip to Storstygge Svånåtinden	Snøheim	17.9	1,075	1,075	7

Åmotdalshytta from Reinheim or Snøheim

29.5 km
18.3 miles

1,030 meters
3,379 feet

1,030 meters
3,379 feet

1-2 days
Challenging

Åmotdalshytta is a small self-service cabin located to the northwest of Snøheim. It's possible to do it as a two day trip, going from Reinheim to Åmotdalshytta to Snøheim. You can also hike directly out and back from either Reinheim or Snøheim.

One option is to go to Åmotdalshytta from Reinheim or Snøheim over Snøhetta. Snøhetta is the highest peak in Norway outside of Jotunheimen, so this is quite a bit of elevation for Norway. The trail starts by following the trail from Reinheim or Snøhiem to Snøhetta. This path involves a lot of climb and plenty of rock hopping until you reach the top of Snøhetta and the weather station. The last section of the climb may have snowfields if you are early in the season.

From here, follow the trail along the ridge and then begin a steep drop down. This is not a popular trail, so some of the markings along the way may be old and difficult to spot. Eventually, the trail reaches the end of the drop and flattens out in high mountain terrain for the last kilometer to the cabin.

An easier option is to go from Snøheim on the western side of Snøhetta. From Snøheim, follow the trail towards the west towards Storstgge Svånådalen. The trail starts in open high mountain terrain and then gests rocky four to five kilometers into the hike. There can be bugs in this section in this summer. The trail climbs up a saddle, then drops down through rocky terrain with a view out onto Langvatnet ("the long lake"). From here, the trail turns northeast to reach Åmotdalshytta.

To return to Snøheim, it's 12 kilometers in rocky terrain on the eastern side of the Snøhetta massiv. It took longer than I expected through this section, and there were still some small snowfields left.

My hiking notes

This was more challenging than I expected from the map but a great hike. The first section of the hike goes through an area that used to be used for shooting practice by the Norwegian military, and when that stopped, the military actually had to come back and clean up spent shells so that musk oxen didn't accidentally eat them.

I did it as a day hike and wouldn't recommend that. It was long enough that I was rushing to get back to dinner at Snøheim, and it would work better spending the night at Åmotdalshytta or even Reinheim.

You can also keep going north here into the Sunndalsøra and even Trollheimen on the DNT trail network.

Summit trip to Storronden

8.5 km
5.3 miles

959 meters
3,146 feet

959 meters
3,146 feet

4 hours
Challenging

This is one of many summit hikes that's doable from Rondvassbu.

From Rondvassbu, follow the marked back towards the east, going up Rondholet. The first section from the cabin is steep. After two kilometers, the trail splits into a section going to Rondeslottet and one going to Storronden. Take the trail towards Storrondonen towards the right. The trail is marked but can be difficult to see through this section. This section is also extremely rocky, so be prepared to scramble.

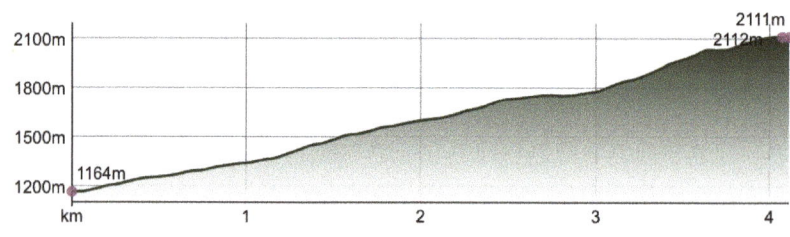

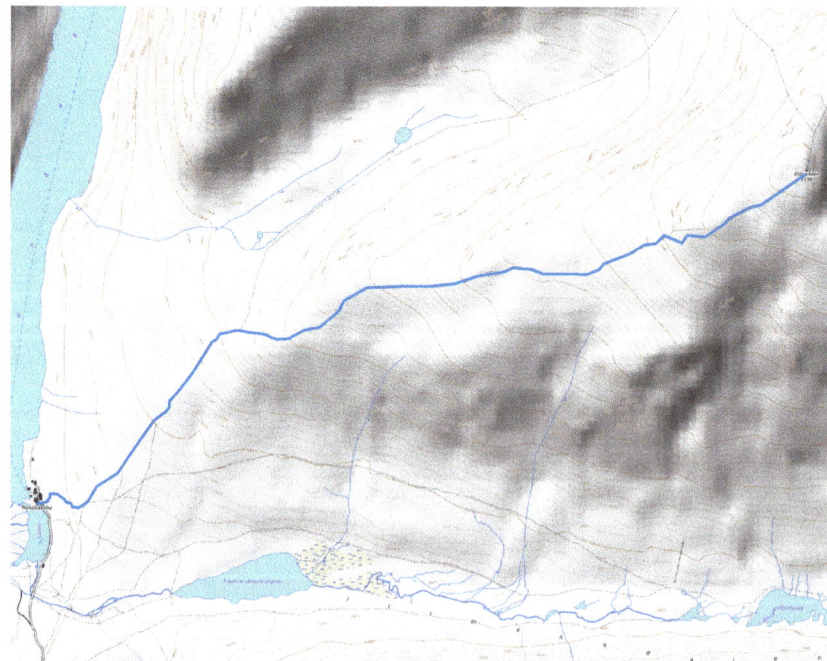

Summit trip to Veslesmeden

11.8 km
7.4 miles

838 meters
2,749 feet

838 meters
2,749 feet

4 hours
Challenging

This is one of many summit hikes that's doable from Rondvassbu. This particular one can be exhausting, particularly in bad weather or with strong wind.

From Rondvassbu, start by going south and then over the bridge over Store Ula. Go past the trails to Smuksjøseter and Høvringen, then turn towards the north up towards Svarthammaren. From here, there is an intense climb up Rondhalsen, then the trail splits. Take the trail towards the northwest and continue the climb up towards the summit. The last few kilometers are very rocky and steep. Reach the summit, then turn around and go back down.

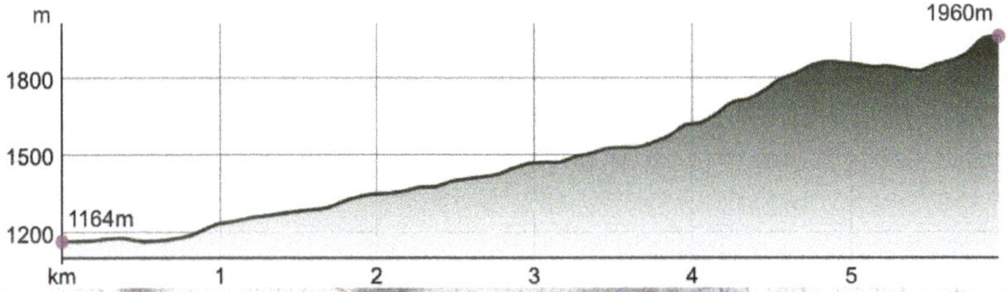

Summit trip to Storstygge Svånåtinden

| 17.9 km | 1,075 meters | 1,075 meters | 7 hours |
| 11.1 miles | 3,527 feet | 3,527 feet | Very challenging |

Like Rondvassbu, Snøheim has a number of fantastic summit tours that can be done as day trips. This one is difficult and should only be done in good weather and good hiking conditions, and only by people who have hiking experience.

From Snøheim, follow the marked trail towards Storstygge Svånåtinden. When you reach the bottom of the mountain, continue on an unmarked path. Follow the path down towards the river Svåni. Cross the river, which will likely require wading. From here, follow the ridge up to the top point of the mountain. This is very steep and has sections that require scrambling over rocks. Reach the top, enjoy the view, and then return the way you came.

If this one feels like a little too much after already doing Saga, you can also do a number of other summit tours in the area. I found the other hikers at dinner to be the best source of information on recommended hikes in the area, because trail conditions depend quite a bit on snow melt and recent rain.

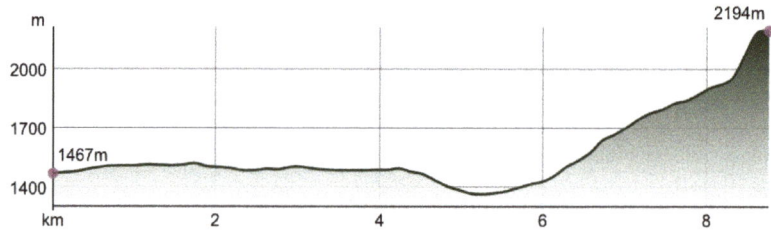

Logistics

Saga is one of the easiest SignaTUR tours to access via public transportation, and as a result, one of the easiest to fit into a shorter trip to Norway.

Getting There and Back

Saga starts from Nordseter, just over Lillehammer. There are about five buses up to Nordseter every day from Lillehammer main station, and you can also take a taxi from the main station to Nordseter. The tourist office in the train station can help with calling taxis, or you can use Lillehammer Taxi's website. The taxi drivers speak English well and will understand badly pronounced Norwegian place names.

There are frequent trains to Lillehammer from Oslo and Oslo airport, but you can save money by booking in advance. The bus ticket to Nordseter doesn't need to be booked in advance and can be bought either via an app, on the bus with a credit card, or at the tourist office.

The shuttle bus from Snøheim back to Hjerkinn Fjellstue can be booked the day of and doesn't need to be booked in advance. I would consider booking the train from Hjerkinn Fjellstue to Oslo in advance because it can sell out during peak travel times, but it's not necessary. Vy.no has train tickets.

It's not necessary to book ahead at any of the DNT cabins. I would recommend not booking ahead unless you're traveling with a group that wants its own room. It gives you more flexibility with the weather. Private cabins may sell out, and you will want to book a day or two in advance for those.

Timing

Rondane and Dovrefjell are located in the east of Norway, and therefore tend to have better weather and faster snow melt than the national parks towards the west. I was able to do Saga with no problem while there was still too much snow to start Massiv, and the weather also tends to be calmer. The only timing issue is that many of the serviced cabins don't open until late June, so check the cabin schedules before booking your flight.

It's worth putting one or two buffer days into the hike in case of bad weather, and there are tons of hikes along the way that you could do as a day trip from one of the cabins.

It's possible to ski Saga as well. The first several days are on either groomed or well-used trails, while the section through Rondane and Dovrefjell is generally marked around the middle of March. If you're planning to ski, definitely check ut.no before you go for the latest on trail status.

Supplies

You can restock on supplies at any of the self-service cabins, and all of the serviced cabins have a place where you can buy basic supplies like band-aids. If you need anything more substantial, like a new pair of shoes or serious gear repair, you're best to take the bus back into Lillehammer, Otta, or Dombås.

Generally, I recommend stocking up in Lillehammer before you go. There are several sports stores in the middle of town, as well as a few grocery stores. The sports stores show up on Google Maps, but look for Coop, Kiwi, or Rema 1000 for the grocery store - for some reason, they don't always show up on Google Maps if you search for "grocery store", but will show up if you search "matbutikk".

Since the first few nights are in self-service cabins, you might also consider bringing some additional food to spice up the offerings. I sometimes take pesto and parmesan to make pasta, cheese or sausage for sandwiches, or chili powder for the prepared foods.

Camping

Norway has some of the most permissive laws in the world around camping. Norway has a law called the Allemannsretten that guarantees the ability of people to explore and experience nature, even in privately owned areas, as long as you're in uncultivated land. Once you're in the wilderness, you may camp in any area, as long as you're at least 150 meters away from the nearest inhabited house or cabin.

Note that the 150 meters applies to the DNT cabins as well - most serviced cabins have marked areas where you can camp, and you'll have to pay a small fee to use the toilets or other common facilities.

Campfires are prohibited everywhere in Norway from April 15 to September 15, except in specifically marked areas in camping sites and by the coast. You will need to bring a gas stove to cook, and in the case of drought, even gas stoves may be banned.

Saga is one of the best SignaTURs to do while camping. The landscapes are generally flat and not too rocky, so it's easy to find places to camp. You can pay for a day visit at one of the cabins if you want to dry off or make food inside.

Planning Resources

UT App and Checking In

In order to be added to the online Hall of Fame for Massiv, you'll need to check in on the UT app (which is sometimes referred to as "SjekkUT", or "check out") at the various cabins or landmarks that you stop at. The UT app only has instructions in Norwegian, so how to do that:

Following a hike – needs to be done in advance:

1. For starters, download the ut app. Once you've downloaded the app, make a profile with your email address and log in on your device.

2. From there, you have to follow the hikes that you want to take. Following the hikes will download the maps around the cabins or areas on that hike, so you'll be able to use them without internet service. This is important.

3. Adding the route to your account is not entirely intuitive. You will need to search for the name of the hike in the search bar. From here, the critical thing is that you follow the list, not the hike. It will be at the bottom of the search results.

4. Click on the list. Make sure it's the one with the list icon. If you click the three dots on the side, you'll get a button that says "Følge", or "follow." Click on that.

5. Congratulations! You have now followed the hike. The maps will download to your phone while you have service.

Checking in:

When you get to a cabin or landmark, you can check in. Click on the icon for the cabin or landmark on the map, and a little green button that says "SjekkUT" will show up on the bottom left. Click on it.

A new screen will pop up. Click on the green button at the bottom again. If you see a screen with confetti, you're checked in!

yr.no is the best resource for weather in Norway. It allows you to hike by specific cabin or mountaintop, with the weather for that particular point rather than the overall area. It's available in English.

Senorge.no shows the current and historic weather conditions for any point in Norway. It's very useful for checking the amount of snow remaining for summer hikes, as well as seeing if it's rained recently.

ut.no is an app and website with detailed maps of Norway with the cabins and trails marked. It's unfortunately only in Norwegian, but is the best source of information on cabins and trails. You can download offline maps by going to "Profil" and then "Mine offline-kart" on the app.

Varsom.no is key for the winter and shows storm and avalanche warnings. It's available in English.

If you're stopping by a DNT office before going hiking, you can pick up a planleggingskart, or planning map. These aren't usable for hiking but are great for planning, since they show the locations of cabins and DNT cabins.

Saga is generally snow free starting in June, unlike many of the other long hikes in Norway.

The weather can be variable in Rondane and Dovrefjell, so I recommend using YR to specifically look up the weather by cabin or mountaintop.

Packing List

In total, the gear below should weigh between 15 and 25 pounds (7 to 12 kilograms).

Gear

□   46-55 liter hiking backpack with a rain shield

□   Maps and compass: *the maps in this guide are overview maps, and I strongly recommend getting 1:50,000 hiking maps just in case you're caught out in low visibility conditions or your phone battery dies.*

□   Hiking poles: *they were super useful for long, flatter sections, snowfields, and river fording for me. I also used them to poke the ground to make sure it was real ground and not just mud*

□   Duct tape

□   Dry bags for packing

□   First aid kit

Clothing

□   Hiking boots

□   Trail runners: *these are optional, but if it's not raining, they'd work well on the first half of Saga. I use mine to give my feet a break from heavy hiking boots*

□   Rain pants and optional gaiters: *in myr or grasses, the water from plants nearby will soak into your pants if you don't have rain pants or gaiters.*

□   Rain jacket

□   Windbreaker: *it's frequently misting in the mornings, so if you don't like hiking in your rain jacket, bring a lighter weight jacket to hike in*

□   Wool socks, two pairs: *I use one pair of socks for hiking and one pair for the cabin.*

□   Hiking shorts (optional): *it may be warm enough to hike in shorts on Saga, but it's very year dependent.*

□   Hiking pants or long underwear to layer under rain pants

□   Two sports bras and two pairs of underwear

□   Wool sweater

□   Extra warm jacket

□   Hat and gloves

□   Two hiking shirts

Rocking the rain jacket even on sunny days - it's handy for keeping out the wind

Cabin Supplies

☐ Mini towel: *for cabins with showers. The showers are usually single gender but communal, so the towel is handy even if you want to create a little shield to get changed under.*

☐ DNT key

☐ Sengetøy (sheet set) or sleep liner: *the blankets on the beds are not washed in between guests. You need to bring your own sheets to keep things clean*

☐ Toilet shoes: *about half of the cabins have outdoor toilets, and this keeps you from having to put potentially wet hiking boots back on*

☐ Sleep mask: *there are good curtains in the cabins, but it never gets dark*

Food and Drink

☐ Thermos for hot drinks

☐ Small plastic water bottle: *there are plenty of rivers and streams to fill up a water bottle as you're hiking*

☐ Candy and snacks

☐ Plastic bag for sandwiches

Tech

☐ Phone: *I recommend downloading UT, YR, and Hyttebetaling before your hike*

☐ Battery pack

☐ Chargers: *many of the cabins only have USB classic charging outlets. If you have a phone with a USB-C charging port, you will want to bring a USB to USB-C charger.*

Other

☐ ID and credit cards: *all of the cabins are payable with the Hyttebetaling app, so there's no need to bring cash*

☐ Sunglasses and sunscreen: *almost the entire hike is unshaded, so if it's sunny, you'll need sunscreen*

☐ Toiletries - wilderness wash, face wash, toothpaste, toothbrush, contacts, contact lens solution, glasses, hairbrush, hair ties, nail clippers, any medications you take as needed

☐ Tiny shovel and toilet paper

☐ Extra plastic bags

Some Handy Norwegian Words

Almost all Norwegians speak perfect English. That said, there are times where it's handy to be able to read signs, the weather, or the map.

Hiking and the map

Bratt/meget bratt: steep/very steep

Breen: the glacier

Dalen: the valley

Grusvei: a gravel path

Luftig: steep drop offs on the side of the trail

Kvistet: marked (used for ski trails)

Merket: marked (used for summer trails)

Mobildekning: phone service

Myr: a swampy, wet land covering

Nord, sor, ost, vest: north, south, east, west

Skog: forest

Stein: rocky

Steinur: rocky patches to hike over

Tind/tinden: peak

Vadested: a place that requires wading

Vannet: the water

Varder: cairns

Vatnet: the lake

Vegen: the road

Weather

Bris: breeze

Flom: flood

Lettskyet: barely cloudy

Lyn: lighting

Nedbør: precipitation

Nysnø: new snow (no icy cover yet)

Regn: rain

Weather continued

Skyet: cloudy

Snø: snow

Sol: sun

Soloppgang, solnedgang: sunrise, sunset

Strynregen: very heavy rain

Tåkete: foggy

Torden: thunder

Things in provision rooms

Bønnemix: mixed beans

Erter: peas

Fullkorn: whole grain

Gryte: stew

Hermetikk: shelf-stable boxes

Kaffe: coffee

Kanel: cinnamon

Kokemalt: coffee that needs to be cooked in a kettle

Kjeks: biscuits

Kjøtt: meat

Knekkebrød: crispbread

Kokk uten lokk: cook without a lid

Kylling: chicken

Lapskaus: a Norwegian stew of potatoes and meat

Legg til: add to (e.g. "legg til vann" = "add water")

Linser: lentils

Melkepulver: milk powder (reconstitute with water)

Ost: cheese

Pannekake: pancakes

Food continued

Potetmos: mashed potatoes

Rein: reindeer

Ror godt: stir well

Smør: butter

Sodd: a high calorie stew of pork, potatoes, and some vegetables

Sukker: sugar

Svine: pork

Syltetøy: jam

Turmat: dehydrated hiking food

Vann: water

Cabins

Betjent: serviced (a lodge)

Selvbetjent: self-service (a cabin without staff but with a provision room)

Ubetjent: unserviced (a cabin with beds, propane, and wood, but no food)

Drikkevann: drinking water

Forhåndsbestilt: booked in advance

Hyttefelt: a collection of cabins

Protokoll: the book you have to sign when you arrive at a cabin

Using the Cabins

One of the most amazing things about hiking in Norway is the national cabin network. The Norwegian Trekking Association (DNT) maintains a network of more than 600 cabins spread across the country. It makes it easy to travel deep into the wilderness without carrying food or a tent.

Cabins come in three grades:

Betjent (serviced):

These aren't cabins but full lodges. You'll have a three course meal for dinner, a buffet breakfast with a place to fill your thermos, showers and drying rooms for clothes, and often indoor toilets.

Dinners are served family style, where the staff will bring out giant tureens of soup for a first course, then usually some kind of meat and potatoes, then individual desserts. There's more than enough food for everyone - but make sure to book ahead and alert the cabin if you have dietary restrictions.

The family style dinners mean that you have to go to an assigned dinner time, usually seven o'clock. There's usually assigned seating. People are generally super friendly at dinner and chat about where you've hiked from that day.

Serviced cabins have electricity, but the number of outlets varies. At many cabins, there are only outlets in the common areas. At others, the electricity is turned off after dinner service ends, so don't rely on an overnight charge for your devices.

Serviced cabins also have drying rooms and showers. Drying rooms usually have strong heaters and dehumidifiers that dry out gear overnight. Showers are usually communal for each gender, so if you're shy, try to go at an off-time.

You'll pack lunch for the next day at breakfast. There is parchment paper and sometimes plastic bags for taking sandwiches in - the Norwegians are generally happy to show you how to wrap a sandwich in parchment paper if you need help. The stay at an serviced cabin also includes a thermos fill up for the next morning - they'll let you know at check in if you should leave your thermos at the reception desk or bring it to breakfast to fill it up yourself.

Selvbetjent (self-service)

Self-service cabins are unique to Norway. They're generally smaller than staffed cabins, but come fully stocked with a provisions room, wood for the fireplace, gas for cooking, and cooking supplies. Some have electricity, but it's usually from a single solar panel and is only enough to charge one or two phones. You usually have to fetch and boil water from a nearby water source.

The self-service cabins run on the honor system. They can be unlocked with the DNT key, which you can purchase at a DNT store in Norway, online at their web store ahead of the hike, or at a staffed cabin. To pay for your stay, use the Hyttebetaling app. The app allows you to keep a list of all the supplies you've used and then pay with credit card when you get back into phone service. The app is available in English.

Ubetjent (unserviced)

These are just like self-service cabins, except that there isn't food available in the provision room. There are no ubetjent cabins on Saga.

Cabin Etiquette:

When you arrive at an unserviced or self-service cabin, the first thing to do is to unlock the cabin and then take off your shoes. No outdoor shoes are allowed in the cabin to help keep it clean. After that, fill in your information in the besøksprotokoll, a horizontal blue book that asks where you came from, where you're going, and your membership information. After that, you have the right to use the cabin. I generally first start a fire if the cabin is cold, then fetch water to heat up for dinner.

When you leave the cabin in the morning, you'll need to clean up. That means washing all of the dishes, cleaning out the ashes in the fireplace, bringing in fresh wood for the fire, washing the floors in the bedroom and common areas, and any other tidying.

You can use the cabins if you're camping. You'll need to register in the besøksprotokoll and pay for a day visit ("dagsbesøk"). After that, you can cook food or just relax for a bit. Make sure to sweep up and wash the floors after yourself.

Cabin FAQs:

It's not necessary to book in advance for the cabins - if you arrive at the cabin, you'll have a place to sleep, though it might be on a mattress on the floor if it's really busy. I generally don't book cabins in advance so that I have the most flexibility possible to change hiking plans based on the weather.

Book ahead at the serviced cabins if you have dietary restrictions. Because meals are served family style, the cabins need advance notice to be able to accommodate dietary restrictions.

Most of the cabins on the Saga route close during the spring for reindeer breeding season. Otherwise, self-serviced and unserviced cabins are generally open year round. UT.no will have information on cabin opening times.

Joining DNT:

You should absolutely join DNT before starting Saga - the savings on staying in the cabin will cover the cost of the membership in two to three nights. If you are planning to camp, you will still want to join DNT to get a DNT key. You'll need the key if you want to do a day visit or if you end up staying in a cabin during a day with particularly bad weather.

Joining online is a little confusing, and there are updated instructions on the blog. You can also stop by any DNT office in Norway.

Cooking at the cabin:

There is a propane stove and plenty of cooking supplies in the cabins. The food that you'll generally find breaks down into four categories:

Breakfast: knekkebrød , oatmeal mixes, pancake mix, leverposti (liver spread), jam and chocolate spread, mackerel in tomatoes, butter, jam, and honey

Dinner: fish soup, peas and carrots, mashed potato mix, lapskaus, rice, bacalo, boxed mixes for Pasta di Parma and Chili Con Carne, pasta, reindeer meatballs, dry red lentils, and crushed tomatoes

Snacks and dessert: chocolate pudding, vanilla sauce, canned fruit in syrup, and biscuits

Misc things: dried hiking food, coffee, tea, hot chocolate, currant drink mix, hiking snacks like knekkebrød sandwiches, sugar, cinnamon

My challenge with cooking at self-service cabins is finding something to bring for lunch the next day. I really load up on breakfast, often mixing vanilla sauce or jam into my oatmeal for the extra calories. I take two or three packages of freeze dried food with me to eat on the trail, in case there isn't shelf-stable cheese and knekkebrød for lunch.

If you don't mind a little extra weight, it can be a good idea to buy some snacks and lunch supplies in Lillehammer before you go. I like taking cheese, crackers, some fresh fruits, and some spices.

Each cabin has a different selection of food, and if you're late in the season, certain items might be eaten up. If you're vegetarian or gluten-free, make sure to have your own backup food

Cabin Overview

Cabin	Cabin Type	Beds	Power
Pellestova	Hotel - private	39	Yes, 220 volt
Djupslia	Self-service	18	Yes, 12 volt
Vetåbu	Self-service	16	Yes, 12 volt
Jammerdalsbu	Self-service	14	No
Veslefjellbu	Self-service	15	Yes, 12 volt
Eldåbu	Self-service	20	Yes, 12 volt
Bjørnhollia	Serviced	90	Yes, 220 volt
Rondvassbu	Serviced	128	Yes, 220 volt
Dørålseter	Hotel - private	100	Yes, 220 volt
Grimdalshytta	Serviced	54	Yes, 220 volt
Hageseter	Hotel - private	70	Yes, 220 volt
Hjerkinn Fjellstue	Hotel - private	70	Yes, 220 volt
Reinheim	Self-service	34	Yes, 12 volt
Snøheim	Serviced	80	Yes, 220 volt

Phone Service	Drying Room	Other Notes	Shower
Yes	Yes	Book in advance	Yes
Yes	Yes		No
No	No		No
No	No		No
Yes	Yes	Recently built	No
No	No		No
No	Yes		Yes
No	Yes	Good spot to spend extra days for summit hies	Yes
Yes, limited	Yes	Had phone service only by flagpole outside	Yes
Yes, limited	Yes		Yes
Yes	Yes	Book in advance	Yes
Yes	Yes	Book in advance	Yes
No	Yes	Smaller self-service cabin	No
Yes	Yes	Good spot to spend extra days for summit hikes	Yes

Saga FAQs

Can I drink the water underway? Do I need to bring a water filter?
You can drink water directly from streams in Norwegian national parks. The cabins also have places where you can fill up water bottles, so no need to bring a water filter.

Where can I leave luggage?
If you have luggage or items that you don't want to bring on the hike, the best place to leave them is either at the Oslo airport or the Lillehammer train station.

The Oslo airport has luggage lockers that you can rent for between $7 and $10/day. Officially, the luggage lockers can only be used for seven days, but if you email hittegods.osl@no.issworld.com and let them know your locker number and plans, there is no problem keeping it there longer.

The Lillehammer train station also has lockers. These also technically have a seven day storage limit, but the tourist information office told me it wouldn't be a problem to use them for longer.

How tough is Saga actually?
Saga is tough because it's a long hike, not because it's technically challenging. I recommend trying the first couple days if you're wondering about it - the first days are technically easy and really helped me get used to hiking.

The same is true with navigation. I took a map and compass as a backup for hiking but was able to just rely on cairns and the UT app.

Is it expensive?
It's about $100/night to stay in a serviced cabin, which includes all food, and $30/night to stay in a self-service cabin. It's a lot cheaper than other hiking trips I've taken because you don't have to pay for a hotel room - you pay by person rather than room. If you want to save on the cost, you can camp some nights rather than staying in the cabins.

Can I rely on the self-service cabins to have food and supplies?
Yes - I've visited 81 DNT cabins so far and have yet to find one that wasn't stocked. If you have dietary restrictions, though, make sure to bring some backup food. There is always food, but it is not always what you're craving.

Fjellvettreglene (Norwegian Mountain Code)

The Norwegian Mountain Code contains the guidelines for having a safe trip in the Norwegian mountains. They're considered an important part of Norwegian cultural heritage and were introduced after a spate of fatal accidents in 1950.

1. Plan your trip and inform others about the route you have selected.

2. Adapt the planned routes according to ability and conditions.

3. Pay attention to the weather and the avalanche warnings.

4. Be prepared for bad weather and frost, even on short trips.

5. Bring the necessary equipment so you can help yourself and others.

6. Choose safe routes. Recognize avalanche terrain and unsafe ice.

7. Use a map and a compass. Always know where you are.

8. Don't be ashamed to turn around

9. Conserve your energy and seek shelter if necessary.

In case of emergency, notify the police at 112. You can also call 911 or 999, and the dispatch will connect you to the correct service. Within the cabins, there are signs giving the coordinates of the cabins and the emergency numbers.

Sarah Rowe has solo hiked more than 3,500 kilometers across 21 countries, with a focus on Norway and Austria. Saga was her first DNT SignaTUR, and she's completed six of them to date.

When she's not out in the mountains, she's drinking coffee, writing about hiking on her blog, Solo Female Wanderer, or planning the next adventure. She lives in the northeastern United States, two kilometers from the Appalachian Trail.

Questions or comments? You can reach her at sarah@solofemalewanderer.com.